High low, high low,

Baby's in the cradle sleeping,

tip toe, tip toe

Still as kitty shyly creeping,

High low, high low,

Rocking the cradle, baby's sleeping,

Hush, my baby, sleep.

Copyright© MCMXCVII MM's Designs
All rights reserved.
No part of this book may be reproduced in any form or
by any means, electronic or mechanical including photocopying,
recording or by any information storage and retrieval system
without the written permission of the publisher.

Published by The C.R. Gibson® Company
Made in China

Lullaby Baby

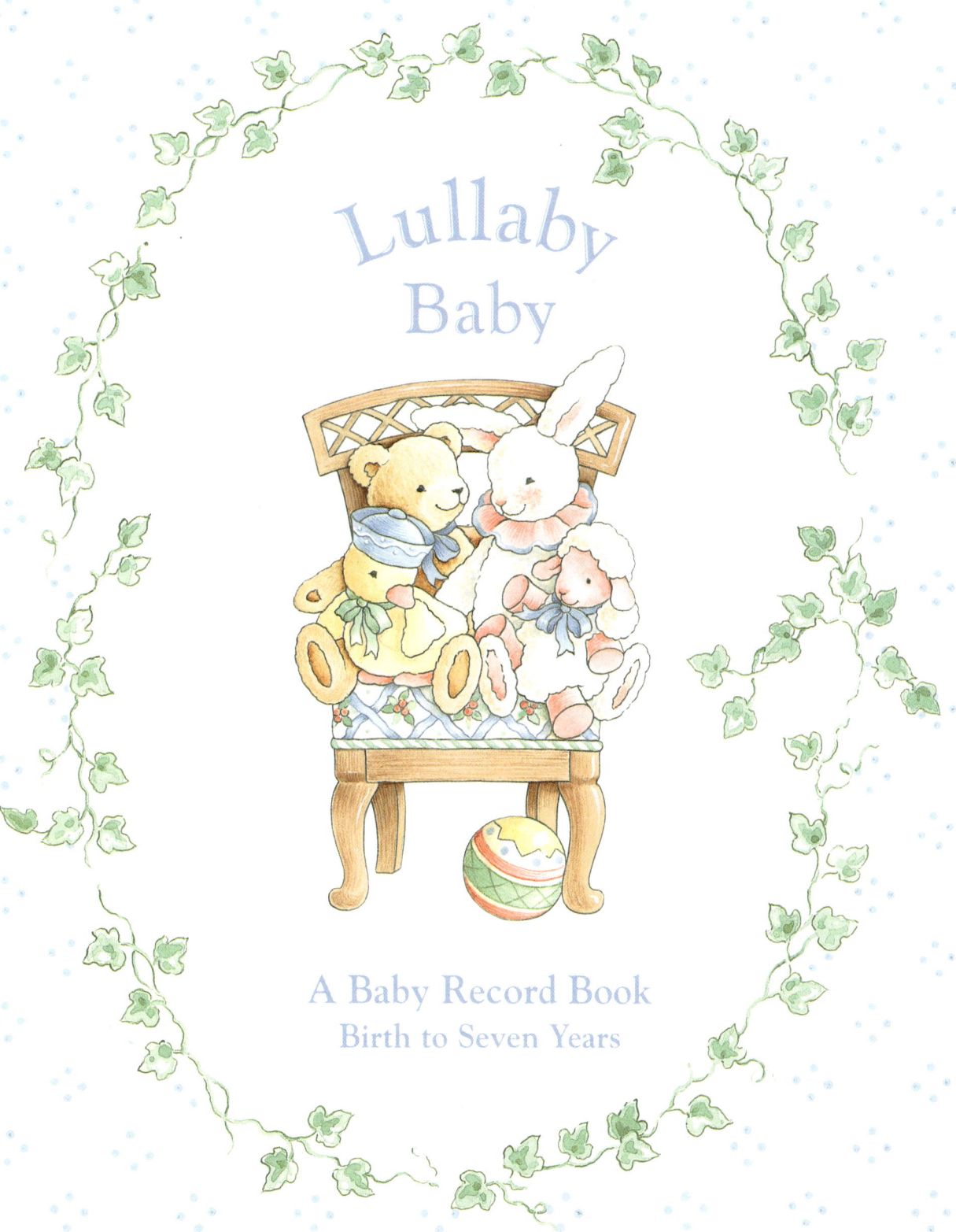

A Baby Record Book
Birth to Seven Years

Published by The C.R.Gibson® Company

Mom's Family

__Veronica__
Grandmother

__Joseph__
Grandfather

_____
Great-grandmother

_____
Great-grandmother

_____
Great-grandfather

_____
Great-grandfather

Dad's Family

__Mary__
Grandmother

__Bill__
Grandfather

_____
Great-grandmother

_____
Great-grandmother

_____
Great-grandfather

_____
Great-grandfather

All About Mom and Dad

Your mother's name Karyn Elizabeth
When and where she was born March 15, 1968
New York

Where she grew up

Her brothers and sisters and their birthdays

Where she was educated

Her occupation
Her talents and hobbies

A description of her

Your father's name Charles Edward
When and where he was born June 26, 1968
Baltimore, Maryland

Where he grew up

His brothers and sisters and their birthdays _____

Where he was educated _____

His occupation _____
His talents and hobbies _____

A description of him _____

When and where your parents met _____

How old they were then __35__
Special memories of their courtship _____

When and where they were married _____

Your Maternal Grandparents

Your maternal grandmother's name _____

When and where she was born _____

_____

Where she grew up _____

_____

Her brothers and sisters and their birthdays _____

_____

Where she was educated _____

_____

Her occupation _____

Her talents and special interests _____

_____

A description of her _____

_____

_____

_____

Your maternal grandfather's name _____

When and where he was born _____

_____

_____

Where he grew up _____

_____

His brothers and sisters and their birthdays _____
_____
_____

Where he was educated _____
_____
_____

His occupation _____
His talents and special interests _____
_____
_____

A description of him _____
_____
_____
_____
_____

When and where your grandparents met _____
_____
_____

Memories of their courtship _____
_____
_____

When and where they married _____
_____

Family traditions they passed down _____
_____
_____
_____
_____

Your Paternal Grandparents

Your paternal grandmother's name _____

When and where she was born _____
_____

Where she grew up _____
_____

Her brothers and sisters and their birthdays _____
_____

Where she was educated _____
_____

Her occupation _____

Her talents and special interests _____
_____
_____

A description of her _____
_____
_____

Your paternal grandfather's name _____

When and where he was born _____
_____

Where he grew up _____
_____

His brothers and sisters and their birthdays

Where he was educated

His occupation

His talents and special interests

A description of him

When and where your grandparents met

Memories of their courtship

When and where they married

Family traditions they passed down

A Dream Come True

My due date May 8, 2005

How I heard the good news

My first reactions

How I told your father

What we did to celebrate

The first people we told

The things they said

How we prepared for your birth _____
_____
_____
_____

Classes we attended _____
_____
_____
_____

Helpful books we read _____
_____
_____
_____

Special advice from family and friends _____
_____
_____
_____
_____

Special baby things you inherited _____
_____
_____
_____

What we wished for you _____

Sleep, my little one sleep. Father is tending the sheep.
Garden and meadow are still, cows are asleep on the hill.
See how the moon rides so high, sailing across the sky.
Time to close your eyes. Sleep my little one, sleep.

Sweet Preparations

My doctor _____

Doctor's address and phone number _____

Special instructions _____

First signs of life _____

When I first heard your heartbeat _____

Prenatal tests _____

Amniocentesis _____

Sonogram _____

Nesting

How I felt about being pregnant _____
_____
_____
_____
_____

My appearance during pregnancy _____
_____
_____
_____
_____

Foods I craved chocolate cake _____
_____
_____
_____

Foods I couldn't eat _____
_____
_____
_____

My age when you were born _____
Your father's age when you were born _____
Special memories of pregnancy _____
_____
_____
_____
_____
_____

Showers of Love

Guests   Gifts

Guests　　　　　　　　Gifts

The Great Day

All about labor _____

When it began *About 3:30 am*

How long it lasted _____

Where you were born *York Hospital*

Who was at the delivery *Daddy and grandmom*

Who delivered you _____

The first thing Mother said when you were born _____

The first thing Father said when you were born _____

We will always remember _____

Baby Is Here

It's a Boy

Day and date of birth Tuesday May 10, 2005
Time 3:13   Color of eyes blue
Weight 7 pounds 4 oz.   Color of hair blonde
Length 19 ½ inches   Blood type

Distinguishing characteristics

Place your first photograph here

A Name So Sweet

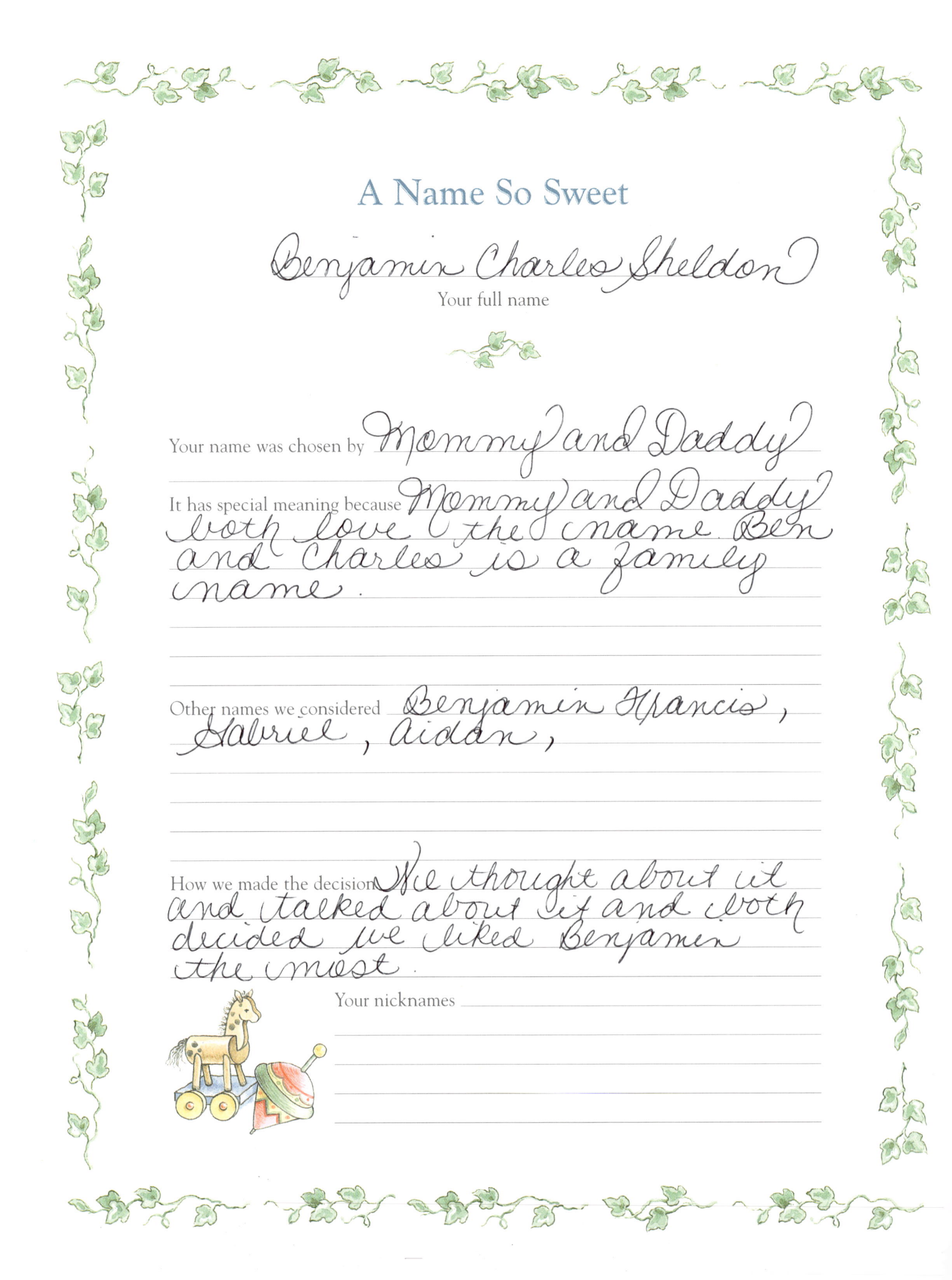

Benjamin Charles Sheldon
Your full name

Your name was chosen by Mommy and Daddy

It has special meaning because Mommy and Daddy both love the name. Ben and Charles is a family name.

Other names we considered Benjamin Francis, Gabriel, Aidan,

How we made the decision We thought about it and talked about it and both decided we liked Benjamin the most.

Your nicknames

First Visitors

Visitors and what they said about you _____

_____

_____

_____

_____

_____

_____

_____

_____

Who they said you looked like _____

_____

_____

_____

_____

_____

_____

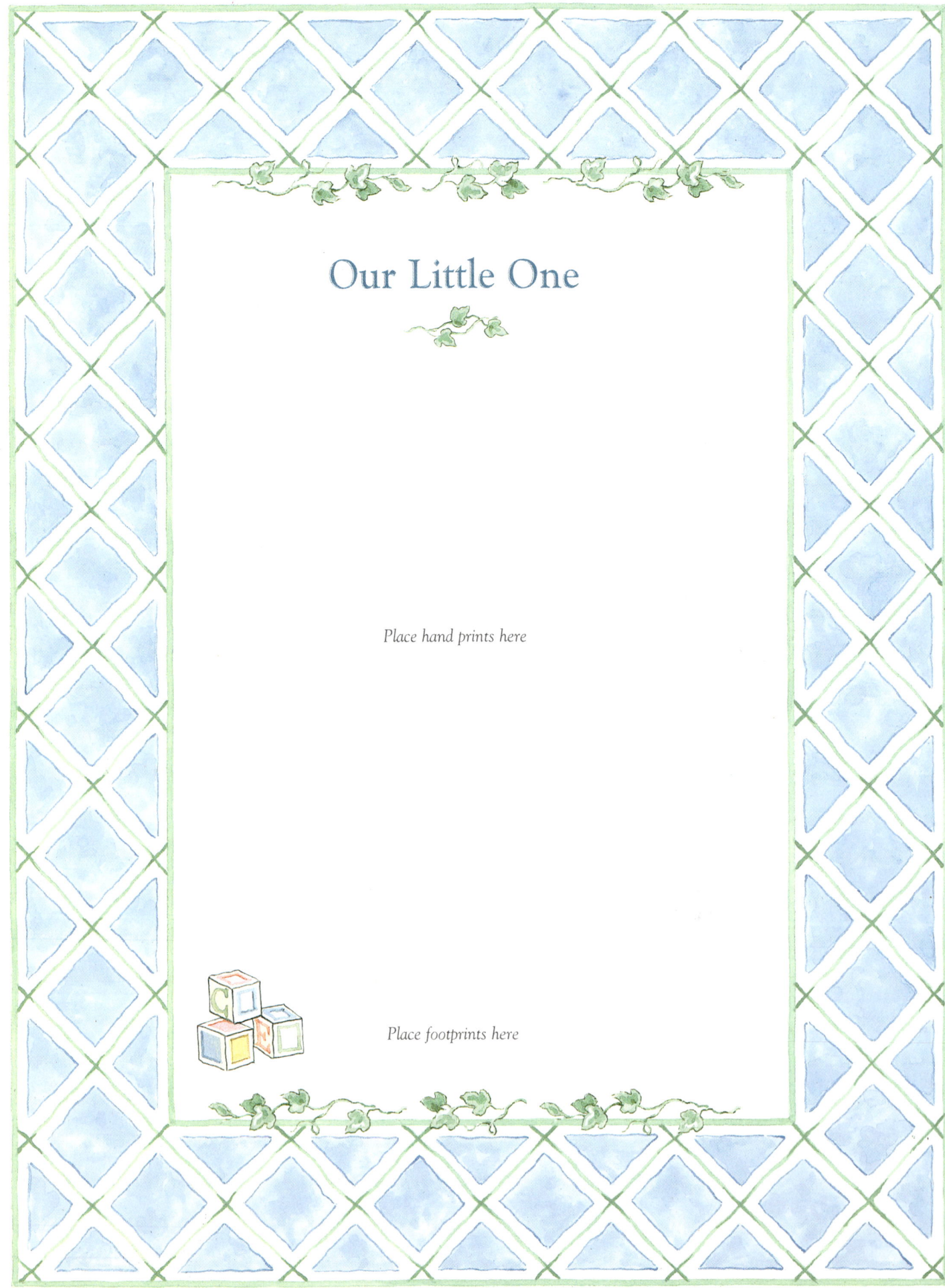

Our Little One

Place hand prints here

Place footprints here

Place a copy of baby's birth certificate here

Place hospital bracelet here

_____
Social Security Number

Telling the World

Place newspaper clippings and announcements here

Place birth announcement here

Smile

Place photograph here

The Big, Bright World

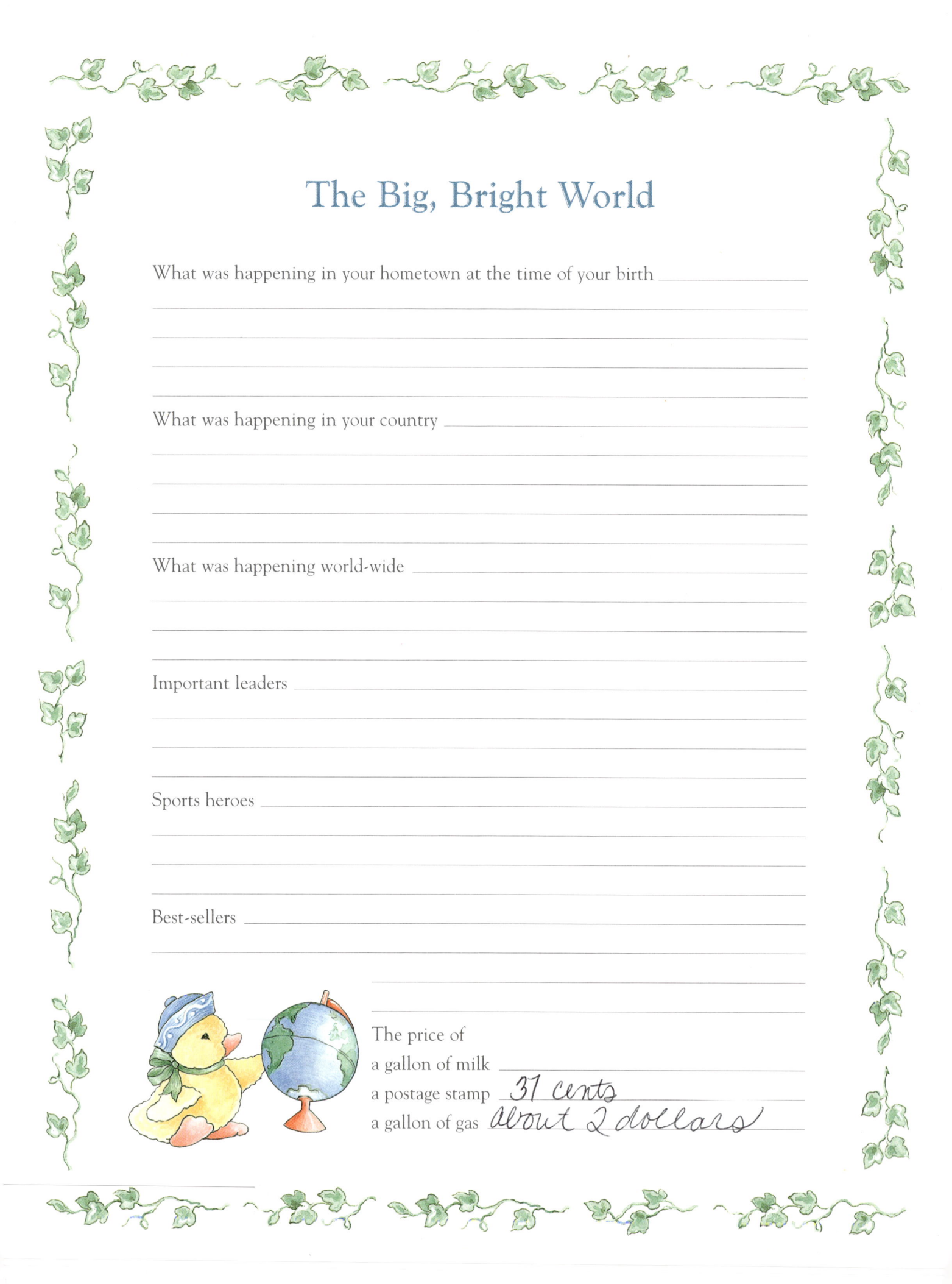

What was happening in your hometown at the time of your birth _____

What was happening in your country _____

What was happening world-wide _____

Important leaders _____

Sports heroes _____

Best-sellers _____

The price of
a gallon of milk _____
a postage stamp *31 cents*
a gallon of gas *about 2 dollars*

Musical groups _____

Popular songs _____

Fashion trends _____

Latest dances _____

Popular movies _____

Broadway shows _____

Hit television shows _____

Favorite stars of stage and screen _____

Snuggling In

Where we lived at the time of your birth _42 Stone Ridge Drive_

Day and date we took you home _Thursday May 12, 2005_
The weather outside _sunny and warm_
Who came to take you home _Daddy_

What you wore _A special blue outfit from grandmom_

Your first reaction to the world outside _____

A description of our home _Our home was filled with a lot of love for Benjamin_

Who was waiting there to greet you _You arrived home to a peacefully quiet home — your brothers were in school_

Siblings _Aaron and Sam_

Pets _____
Who helped take care of you _Mommy, Daddy, Aaron, and Sam_

Rock me slowly up the stairs
To snuggle down with my teddy bears.
Rock me easy, rock me slow,
Rock me where the robins go.

Place picture of nursery here

How your nursery was decorated *western*

Our first days at home together *were exciting for aaron & sam and mommy & daddy*

Some moments we'll never forget

Family and Friends

Visitors and the gifts they brought:
_____
_____
_____
_____
_____
_____
_____
_____
_____
_____
_____
_____
_____
_____
_____
_____
_____

For the First Time

The first time you...
- slept through the night _____
- held a bottle _____
- turned over _____
- crawled _____
- wore shoes _____
- sat unsupported _____
- stood up _____
- took first step with help _____
- took first step alone _____
- started to walk _____
- held a cup _____
- ate solid food _____
- said a word _____
- bathed in tub _____
- held a spoon _____
- spoke a sentence _____
- brushed teeth _____
- sat on your potty _____
- stopped wearing diapers _____
- drew a picture _____
- sang a song _____
- made a friend _____
- other _____

_____
_____
_____
_____
_____
_____

More Firsts

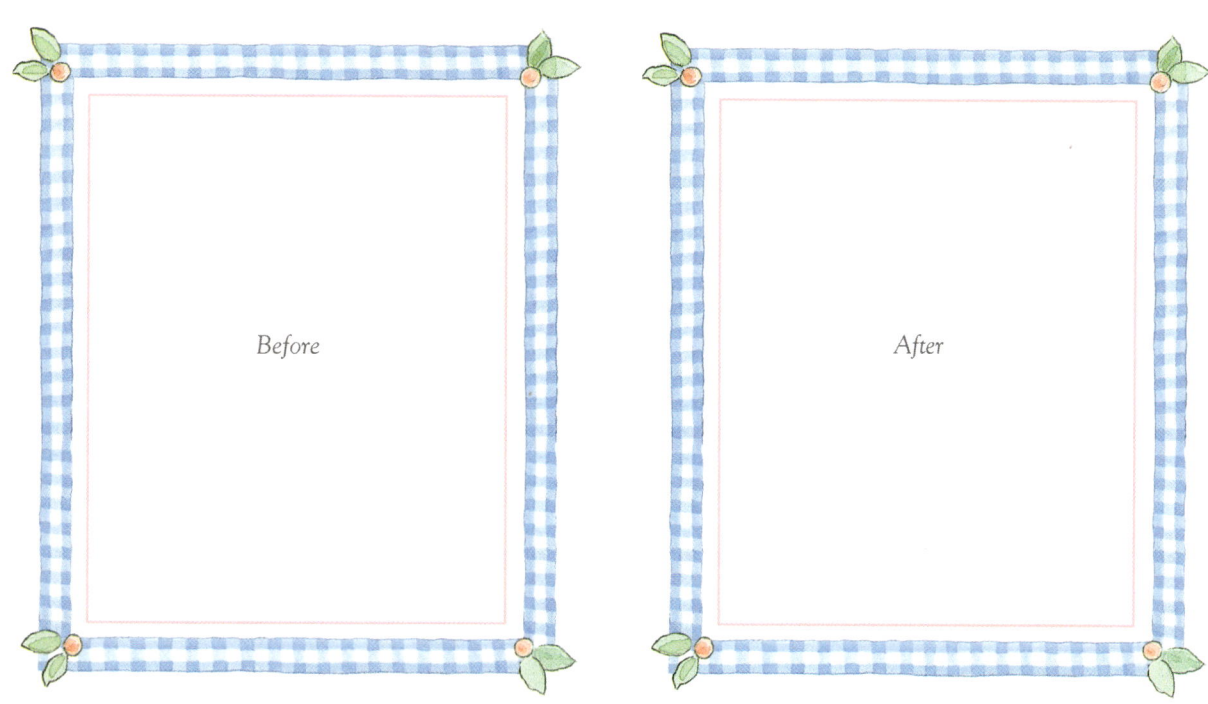

Before　　　　　　　　　　*After*

First haircut
Your barber's name _____
When and where _____
_____
_____

Your reaction _____
_____
_____

Autographs
　At age 1 _____
　At age 2 _____
　At age 3 _____
　At age 4 _____
　At age 5 _____
　At age 6 _____
　At age 7 _____

Sugar and Spice

As a baby you were

Your feeding patterns

Your sleeping patterns

You laughed when

You cried when

Your reaction to strangers

Your favorite sayings

Your funniest mispronunciations

Special things you did

And Everything Nice

As you grew older…

Your favorite foods _____
_____

Foods you pushed away _____
_____

Your best-loved toys _____

Your favorite games _____

Stories and rhymes you loved to hear _____
_____

Songs you sang _____

Television shows you watched _____
_____
_____

Your favorite movie _____
Your favorite people _____
Your favorite "dress up" clothes _____
Your Halloween costumes
    Age 1 _____
    Age 2 _____
    Age 3 _____
    Age 4 _____
    Age 5 _____
    Age 6 _____
    Age 7 _____

Sunny Days

Where you slept as a new baby *You slept with mommy and daddy*

How you slept

How we put you back to sleep when you woke *Usually you nursed back to sleep*

Nighttime feedings/breast or bottle *Breast feedings were about every 2-3 hours*

Preparations for bedtime *Bath time*

When you first slept through the night
Napping schedule

Your moods when you woke

When you moved from crib to bed

*Lullaby and good night,
see stars shining bright.
Rock gently, rock slow,
to Dreamland you go.*

Starry Nights

When you got older your bedroom looked _____

_____

_____

Who put you to bed at night _____

How we prepared you for sleep _____

_____

Favorite bedtime stories _____

_____

Favorite sleep toy _____

_____

Favorite lullaby or music _____

What you wore to bed _____

_____

Your famous excuses for getting out of bed _____

_____

Sweet dreams _____

_____

Night fears _____

_____

*In my arms you will sleep,
ever close to me.
May your dreams be sweet,
as you drift off to sleep.*

Exploring Baby's World

Where we went on our walks

Your first trip to visit relatives

Your favorite day trips

How you acted in the car

Eating out

What we did on weekends

Your first train or plane ride

How you reacted to new surroundings…

At the beach _____

In the snow _____

In the woods _____

Your first overnight away from us _____

Your favorite outdoor activity _____

Wonderful One

Place first birthday photo here

How we celebrated your First Birthday _____
_____
_____
_____

Guests & Gifts
_____
_____
_____
_____

Second Birthday

Place photo here

How we celebrated your Second Birthday _____

_____
_____
_____
_____
_____

Guests & Gifts

_____
_____
_____

Third Birthday

How we celebrated your Third Birthday _____

_____
_____
_____
_____
_____

Guests & Gifts

_____
_____
_____

Place photo here

Fourth Birthday

How we celebrated your Fourth Birthday _____

Guests & Gifts

Place photo here

Fifth Birthday

Place photo here

How we celebrated your Fifth Birthday _____

Guests & Gifts

Sixth Birthday

Place photo here

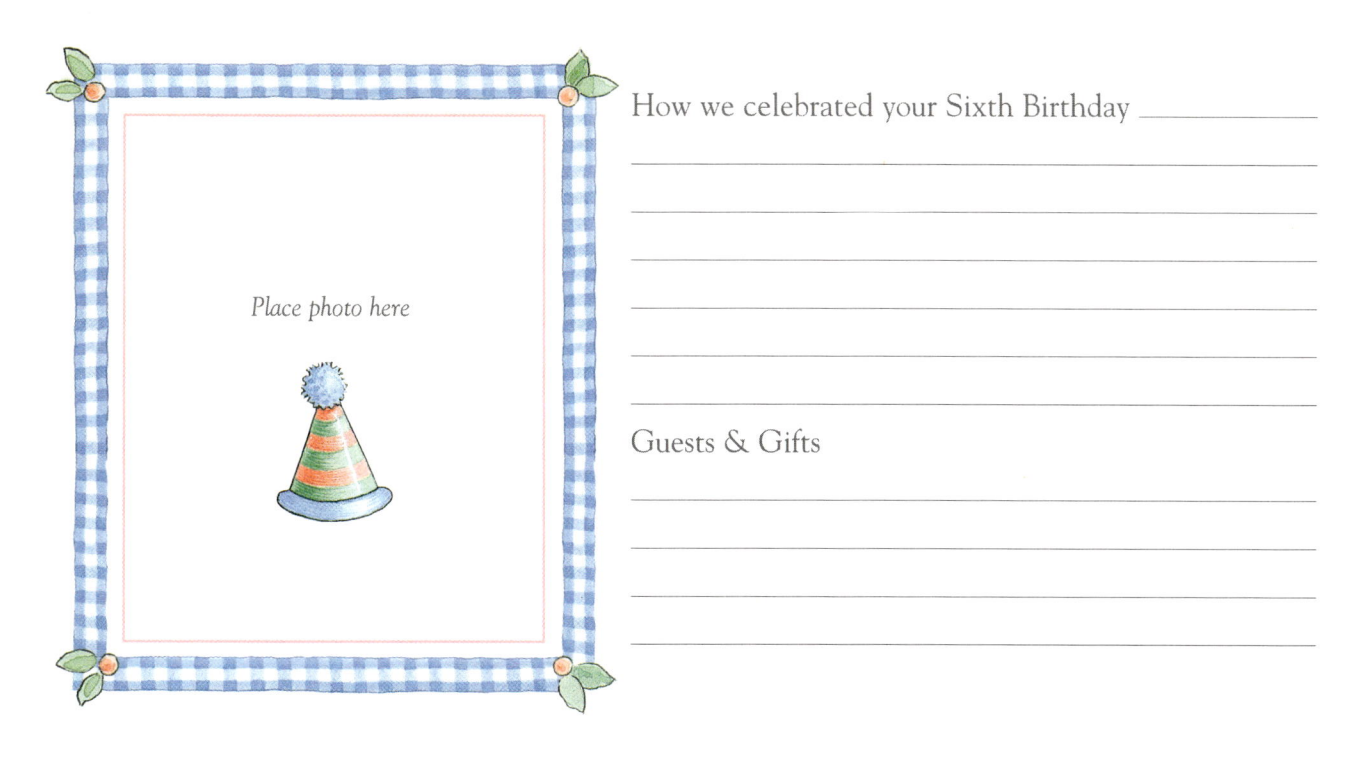

How we celebrated your Sixth Birthday _____

_____
_____
_____
_____
_____
_____

Guests & Gifts

_____
_____
_____
_____

Seventh Birthday

How we celebrated your Seventh Birthday _____

_____
_____
_____
_____
_____

Guests & Gifts

_____
_____
_____

Place photo here

First Holidays

First Holidays

Special Occasions

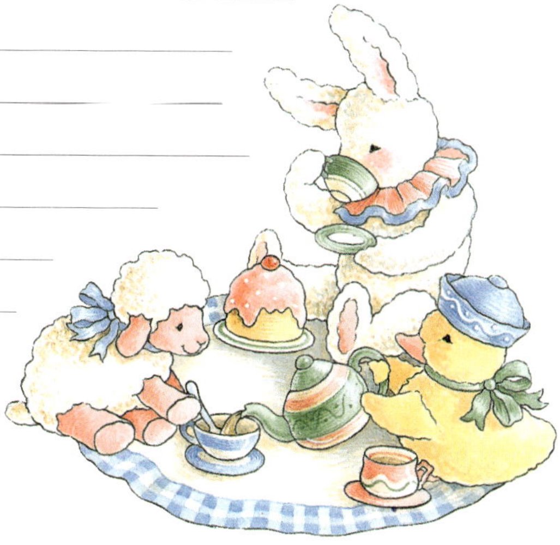

Caring For You

Who took care of you during the day

How you spent your days

Friends you played with

Playgroups

Special time with Mother

Special time with Father

Favorite baby-sitters

Preschool

The name of your preschool _____

_____

The address _____

_____

Your teacher's name _____

What happened when you left on your first day _____

_____

_____

The friends you made _____

_____

_____

Accomplishments _____

_____

_____

_____

Special lessons and classes _____

_____

_____

After school play _____

_____

_____

Off To School

Elementary School

Address

What happened on your first day

How we felt

How you felt

Kindergarten

Your teacher
The friends you made

Your favorite subjects

Your special accomplishments

Your report card
Playdates

First Grade

Your teacher _____

The friends you made _____

_____

Your favorite subjects _____

_____

Your special accomplishments _____

_____

Your report card _____

Playdates _____

_____

Second Grade

Your teacher _____

The friends you made _____

_____

Your favorite subjects _____

_____

Your special accomplishments _____

_____

Your report card _____

Playdates _____

_____

Precious Baby

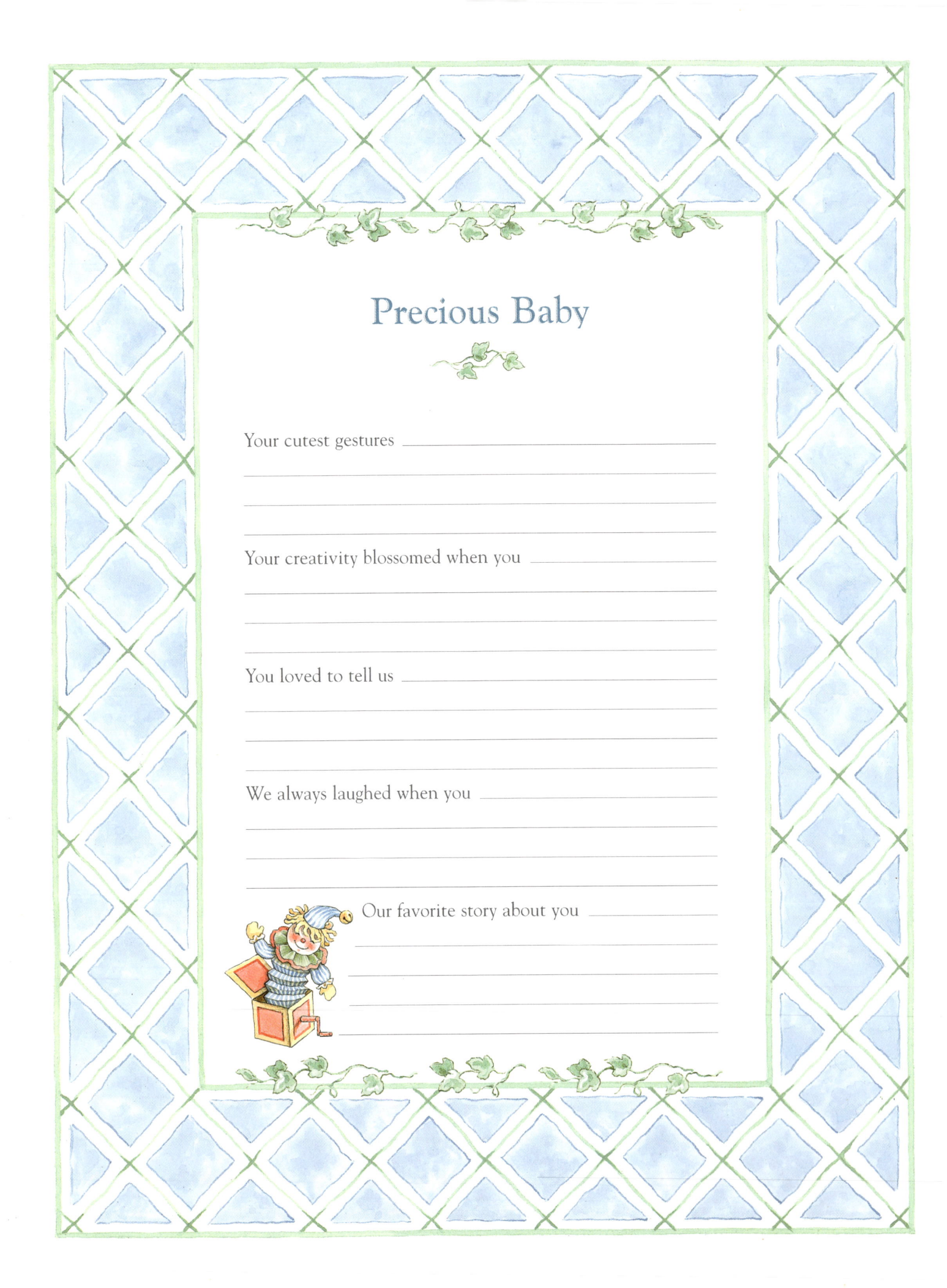

Your cutest gestures _____
_____
_____
_____

Your creativity blossomed when you _____
_____
_____
_____

You loved to tell us _____
_____
_____
_____

We always laughed when you _____
_____
_____
_____

Our favorite story about you _____
_____
_____
_____

Your Masterpieces

Draw or place artwork here

A Letter from Mom

A Letter from Dad

As You Grew...

Date	Age	Height	Weight
5-10-05	newborn	19 ½ in	7 lb. 4 oz.
5- -05	2 weeks		
6- -05	1 month		10 lb 6 oz.

Your Health

Immunizations		Date	Reaction
Diphtheria Tetanus Pertussis	DTP:		
Oral Polio Vaccine	OPV:		
Measles Mumps Rubella	MMR:		
Haemophilus	HIB:		
Hepatitis B:		5-11-05 6- -05	you cried - daddy held you you cried - daddy snuggled you
Other:			

Illnesses

Date Treatment and Comments

Open Wide

Your dentist _____
Your first visit _____
Your reaction _____
_____

Dates teeth first appeared

	Left	Right
1. Central Incisor	_____	_____
2. Lateral Incisor	_____	_____
3. Cuspid	_____	_____
4. First Molar	_____	_____
5. Second Molar	_____	_____
5. Second Molar	_____	_____
4. First Molar	_____	_____
3. Cuspid	_____	_____
2. Lateral Incisor	_____	_____
1. Central Incisor	_____	_____

Upper

Lower

Dental Check-ups

Age	Date	Treatment
_____	_____	_____
_____	_____	_____
_____	_____	_____
_____	_____	_____
_____	_____	_____
_____	_____	_____
_____	_____	_____

Golden Slumbers kiss your eyes,

Smiles awake you when you rise.

Sleep, pretty children, do not cry,

And I will sing a lullaby.

Lullaby, lullaby, lullaby.